MOM & ME

A JOURNAL FOR MOTHERS AND DAUGHTERS

Ruby Oaks

CASTLE POINT BOOKS

NEW YORK

MOM & ME. Copyright © 2020 by St. Martin's Press.
All rights reserved. Printed in Singapore. For information,
address St. Martin's Press, 120 Broadway, New York, NY 10271.

www.castlepointbooks.com

The Castle Point Books trademark is owned by Castle Point Publications, LLC.
Castle Point books are published and distributed by St. Martin's Press.

ISBN 978-1-250-25956-1

Cover design by Katie Jennings Campbell
Interior design by Joanna Williams

Images used under license from Shutterstock.com

Our books may be purchased in bulk for promotional, educational, or business use.
Please contact your local bookseller or the Macmillan Corporate
and Premium Sales Department at 1-800-221-7945, extension 5442.

First Edition: April 2020

10 9 8 7 6 5 4 3 2 1

INTRODUCTION

OUR HEARTS AND MINDS ARE OFTEN FILLED with so many things we're not quite sure how to share in conversation. Even the closest mothers and daughters face this challenge. That's why this journal offers a special place to discover more about each other, bring up tough topics that could be awkward face to face, support each other when you can't be together in person, reveal your hopes and dreams for the future, and just plain have fun celebrating the unique individuals you are and the love and laughter you share together.

As you begin your back-and-forth journaling experience, discuss the ground rules. Here are a few suggestions to get you started:

KEEP this journal just between you. Make a promise to keep the contents in this book private.

AGREE on a way to say, "I'm not ready to talk about this beyond the journal pages—yet." Maybe it's drawing a padlock symbol or writing "stays here" next to that entry.

ACCEPT that doodles are as good as words. Sometimes drawings can say what words can't.

CREATE a no-judgment zone where there are no right and wrong answers (only honest ones), and spelling and grammar don't need to be perfect.

PROMISE to always write back within a reasonable amount of time. If you poured out your soul and it needs urgent attention, flag the page with a piece of paper that says "read me."

With each pass of this journal between your hands and hearts, you'll be reminded of the special, ever-growing connection you have. And when the pages are full, save *Mom & Me* as a time capsule of your relationship and a celebration of all you can do together.

TOGETHER TIME
MOTHER

My favorite memory of us together:

....

....

I love this photo of us:

My perfect caption: _____

(*Dear Daughter*
Fill in *your* perfect caption:)

What I'm looking forward to as we begin this journal:

....

TOGETHER TIME
DAUGHTER

My favorite memory of us together:

....

....

I love this photo of us:

My perfect caption: _____

Dear Mom
Fill in *your* perfect caption:

What I'm looking forward to as we begin this journal:

....

ALL ABOUT ME
MOTHER

A sight that makes me happy: ....

A scent that makes me happy: ....

My favorite movie: ....

My favorite song: ....

My favorite book: ....

Something I collect: ....

The one food I could eat anytime: ....

The best gift I ever received: ....

Something I recently learned: ....

A place I want to go someday: ....

[
Dear Daughter
What surprised you most?
]

ALL ABOUT ME
DAUGHTER

A sight that makes me happy: ....

A scent that makes me happy: ....

My favorite movie: ....

My favorite song: ....

My favorite book: ....

Something I collect: ....

The one food I could eat anytime: ....

The best gift I ever received: ....

Something I recently learned: ....

A place I want to go someday: ....

Dear Mom
What surprised you most?

DATE:

LET'S DO IT!
MOTHER

Ten things (big or little) I'd like us to do together in the next year:

1. ....
2. ....
3. ....
4. ....
5. ....
6. ....
7. ....
8. ....
9. ....
10. ....

Dear Daughter
Put a star next to the ones you'd like to do first.

LET'S DO IT!
DAUGHTER

Ten things (big or little) I'd like us to do together in the next year:

1. ....

2. ....

3. ....

4. ....

5. ....

6. ....

7. ....

8. ....

9. ....

10. ....

Dear Mom
Put a star next to the ones you'd like to do first.

TOUGH STUFF
MOTHER

Something I find difficult to do:

....

....

....

One of my biggest fears:

....

....

....

What makes me feel better when I'm going through a hard time:

....

....

....

BE
BRAVE

Dear Daughter
What do you think makes a person strong?

TOUGH STUFF
DAUGHTER

Something I find difficult to do:

....

....

....

One of my biggest fears:

....

....

....

What makes me feel better when I'm going through a hard time:

....

....

....

Dear Mom
When do you see me being strong?

YOU CAN

LOOKING BACK
MOTHER

What I loved to do as a kid:

....

....

What I wanted to be when I grew up:

....

....

....

A special childhood day I remember:

....

....

Dear Daughter
What's a special day that stands out in your memory?

LOOKING FORWARD
DAUGHTER

A day in the near future that I'm excited about:

....

....

....

What I'm looking forward to about growing up:

....

....

....

What I'm a little unsure of about growing up:

....

....

Dear Mom
What's one way I am like or unlike you as a kid?

I SAY, YOU SAY
MOTHER

Actor who would play me in a movie: ....

A song that describes my room: ....

Three things I am good at: ....

....

....

One thing I'm terrible at (but I don't care): ....

What makes me laugh: ....

The best thing I can make: ....

If I were an animal, I would be: ....

Something I always say: ....

Type of store I should open: ....

My superhero name: ....

Dear Daughter
Write your entries about me next to mine.

I SAY, YOU SAY
DAUGHTER

Actor who would play me in a movie: ....

A song that describes my room: ....

Three things I am good at: ....

....

....

One thing I'm terrible at (but I don't care): ....

What makes me laugh: ....

The best thing I can make: ....

If I were an animal, I would be: ....

Something I always say: ....

Type of store I should open: ....

My superhero name: ....

No DRama LLama!

MOOOOD

Dear Mom
Write your entries about me next to mine.

TALKING POINTS
MOTHER

What I talked about with my mom when I was your age:

....
....
....
....

HELLO
YOU

What I wish I'd been able to talk about with her:

....
....
....

What I want you to feel comfortable talking about with me:

....
....
....

[
Dear Daughter
Is there a place you feel most comfortable talking to me?
]

TALKING POINTS
DAUGHTER

What I like talking about with you:

....

....

....

HI

What I find hard to talk about with you:

....

....

....

What makes opening up easier for me:

....

Hello

....

....

....

Dear Mom
If you're ever not available, who else could I talk to?

DATE:

KIND OF A BIG DEAL
MOTHER

The last kind act someone did for me:

....
....
....
....

The last kind act I did for someone else:

....
....
....
....

Something kind I've spotted you doing:

....
....
....
....

Dear Daughter
When do you need me to be especially kind to you?

18

KIND OF A BIG DEAL
DAUGHTER

The last kind act someone did for me:

....
....
....
....

The last kind act I did for someone else:

....
....
....
....

Something kind I've spotted you doing:

....
....
....
....

Dear Mom
What kind little thing can I do for you?

PLACES & SPACES
MOTHER

What I liked about where I grew up:

....

....

....

What I would have changed about my hometown:

....

....

....

....

My favorite space in our home now:

....

....

....

Dear Daughter
Where would you like to go on a mother-daughter day?

PLACES & SPACES
DAUGHTER

What I like about where we live now:

....

....

....

My favorite place in our town:

....

....

....

....

Where I would like to live someday:

....

....

....

Dear Mom
What special place do you want me to see someday?

REWIND TIME
MOTHER

What I wish had gone differently this week:

....

....

....

What I miss that we used to do:

....

....

....

....

An odd day we had together that turned out pretty wonderful:

....

....

....

Dear Daughter
What step are you glad you got over the fear of taking?

REWIND TIME
DAUGHTER

What I wish had gone differently this week:

....

....

....

What I miss that we used to do:

....

....

....

An odd day we had together that turned out pretty wonderful:

....

....

....

NEW day

Dear Mom

What's something you were afraid of when you were a kid?

23

CLASS ACT
MOTHER

My favorite parts of the day when I was in school:

....

....

My least favorite parts of the day when I was in school:

....

....

....

Teachers or coaches who influenced my life:

....

....

....

[*Dear Daughter*
What class could we take together?]

CLASS ACT
DAUGHTER

My perfect school day would include lots of:

....

....

....

MY UNICORN
ate my
HOMEWORK

But we would skip:

....

....

....

The currently nonexistent clubs or teams I would love to start:

....

....

....

Dear Mom
What class could you see me teaching someday?

DATE:

WOULD YOU RATHER?
MOTHER

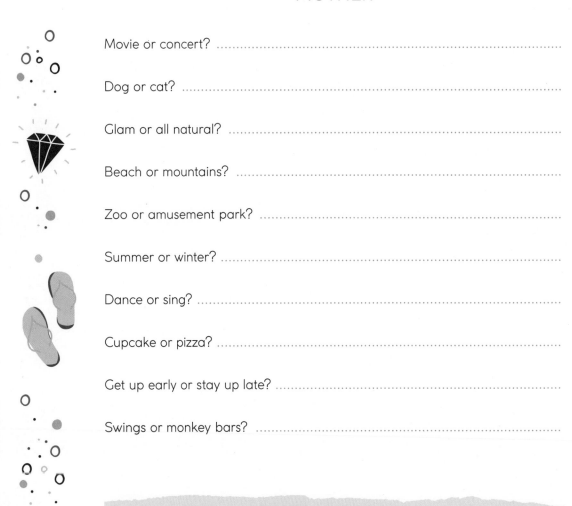

Movie or concert? ....

Dog or cat? ....

Glam or all natural? ....

Beach or mountains? ....

Zoo or amusement park? ....

Summer or winter? ....

Dance or sing? ....

Cupcake or pizza? ....

Get up early or stay up late? ....

Swings or monkey bars? ....

Dear Daughter
_____ or _____?
Circle your answer for the choices I have written in.

WOULD YOU RATHER?
DAUGHTER

Movie or concert? ....

Dog or cat? ....

Glam or all natural? ....

Beach or mountains? ....

Zoo or amusement park? ....

Summer or winter? ....

Dance or sing? ....

Cupcake or pizza? ....

Get up early or stay up late? ....

Swings or monkey bars? ....

Dear Mom

_____ or _____?

Circle your answer for the choices I have written in.

DATE:

UPS AND DOWNS
MOTHER

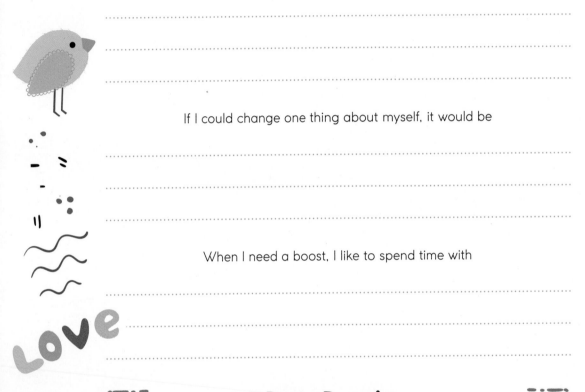

I feel on top of the world when

....
....
....

If I could change one thing about myself, it would be

....
....
....

When I need a boost, I like to spend time with

....
....
....

Love

Dear Daughter
When have you felt proud of me?

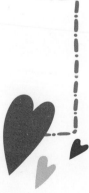

28

UPS AND DOWNS
DAUGHTER

I feel on top of the world when

If I could change one thing about myself, it would be

When I need a boost, I like to spend time with

Dear Mom
When have you felt proud of me?

IN YOUR DREAMS
MOTHER

Dream job: ....

Dream vacation: ....

Dream celebrity meeting: ....

Dream talent: ....

Dream wardrobe: ....

Dream meal: ....

Dream superpower: ....

Dream house: ....

Dream car: ....

Dream way to spend a day: ....

Dear Daughter
What was the last crazy dream you had?

[   ]

IN YOUR DREAMS
DAUGHTER

Dream job: ....

Dream vacation: ....

Dream celebrity meeting: ....

Dream talent: ....

Dream wardrobe: ....

Dream meal: ....

Dream superpower: ....

Dream house: ....

Dream car: ....

Dream way to spend a day: ....

Dear Mom
What did you dream about when you were my age?

PLAYING BY THE RULES
MOTHER

The household or school rule I had the most trouble following as a kid:

....

....

....

A time I got into trouble at home or school:

....

....

....

....

The people who kept me out of trouble most of the time:

....

....

....

Dear Daughter
Do you think it was easier to grow up when I did or now?

PLAYING BY THE RULES
DAUGHTER

The household or school rule I would most like to change:

....

....

....

A new household or school rule I think we should make:

....

....

....

....

The people who keep me out of trouble most of the time:

....

....

....

Dear Mom
How are you like or unlike your parents when it comes to rules?

BEAUTIFUL THINGS
MOTHER

Through words, drawings, and/or photos, cover this page
with things you consider beautiful.

Dear Daughter
What do you think makes something beautiful?

_____

BEAUTIFUL THINGS
DAUGHTER

Through words, drawings, and/or photos, cover this page
with things you consider beautiful.

Dear Mom
What's the most beautiful thing you've ever seen?

YOU NAME IT
MOTHER

The history of my name:

....
....
....

Why I like it or don't:

....
....
....

Nicknames people have for me:

....
....
....

Dear Daughter

What nicknames do you like me to call you—
and which make you cringe?

YOU NAME IT
DAUGHTER

If I could have chosen my name:

....

....

....

Why I like my name or don't:

....

....

....

Nicknames people have for me:

....

....

....

Dear Mom
How did you choose my name?

SPECIAL DAYS
MOTHER

One of the best days of my life:

....

....

....

....

My favorite holiday:

....

....

....

My favorite family tradition:

....

....

....

Dear Daughter
If you could invent a new holiday, what would it be?

SPECIAL DAYS
DAUGHTER

One of the best days of my life:

....

....

....

....

My favorite holiday:

....

....

....

My favorite family tradition:

....

....

....

....

Dear Mom
What day in your life would you like to travel back to?

ONE OF A KIND
MOTHER

DREAMER

Three words that describe me:

1. ....

2. ....

3. ....

Three ways in which I'm unique:

1. ....

2. ....

3. ....

Three things I love about myself:

1. ....

2. ....

3. ....

[*Dear Daughter*
What three words do you think describe me?]

ONE OF A KIND
DAUGHTER

Three words that describe me:

1. ....

2. ....

3. ....

free soul

Three ways in which I'm unique:

1. ....

2. ....

3. ....

Three things I love about myself:

1. ....

2. ....

3. ....

Dear Mom
What three words do you think describe me?

41

HIGH HOPES
MOTHER

If I wrote a book, it would be about

....
....
....

If I could solve a world problem, it would be

....
....
....
....

If I could meet anyone (alive or dead), it would be

....
....
....

Dear Daughter
What are you hoping will happen this year?

HIGH HOPES
DAUGHTER

If I wrote a book, it would be about

....

....

....

If I could solve a world problem, it would be

....

....

....

If I could meet anyone (alive or dead), it would be

....

....

....

Dear Mom
What hopes do you have for me in the next year?

QUESTIONS & ANSWERS
MOTHER

Something I know for sure:

....

....

....

Questions I still have:

....

....

....

....

I get the best advice from:

....

....

....

WHAT

?

?

?

WHEN

Dear Daughter
Is there anything you want my advice on right now?

QUESTIONS & ANSWERS
DAUGHTER

Something I know for sure:

....

....

....

Questions I still have:

....

....

....

....

WHY

?

I get the best advice from:

....

....

....

WHERE

Dear Mom
What's the best mistake you ever made?

PERFECT TIMING
MOTHER

Something I wish would last forever:

....
....
....
....

Something I want to end:

....
....
....

Something that's perfect just the way it is right now:

....
....
....
....

Dear Daughter
What seems to be taking too long in your life?

PERFECT TIMING
DAUGHTER

Something I wish would last forever:

....

....

....

....

Something I want to end:

....

....

....

Something that's perfect just the way it is right now:

....

....

....

....

Dear Mom
What seemed like the longest day of your life?

GREAT PAIRS
MOTHER

A famous duo we're like: ....

A meal combo I love: ....

My favorite pair of shoes: ....

A couple I admire: ....

My best friend: ....

My favorite pair of jeans: ....

My favorite movie with a sequel: ....

Two flowers I'd mix in a bouquet: ....

My favorite color combo: ....

Favorite ice cream and topping: ....

Dear Daughter
How do you think we're alike?

GREAT PAIRS
DAUGHTER

A famous duo we're like: ....

A meal combo I love: ....

My favorite pair of shoes: ....

A couple I admire: ....

My best friend: ....

My favorite pair of jeans: ....

My favorite movie with a sequel: ....

Two flowers I'd mix in a bouquet: ....

My favorite color combo: ....

Favorite ice cream and topping: ....

Dear Mom
What was the first day we spent together like?

FAMILY MATTERS
MOTHER

What I love about our family:

....

....

....

Something I wish I could change about our family:

....

....

....

How our family is what I pictured growing up and how it was a surprise:

....

....

....

Dear Daughter
What's your favorite family activity?

FAMILY MATTERS
DAUGHTER

What I love about our family:

....

....

....

Something I wish I could change about our family:

....

....

....

....

The kind of family I want when I grow up:

....

....

....

Dear Mom
What was your favorite family activity when you were growing up?

EVERYDAY FUN
MOTHER

The last place I went: ....

The last photo I took: ....

The last song I heard: ....

The last TV show/movie I watched: ....

What I'm wearing right now: ....

The last person I talked to: ....

The last emoji I used: ....

Something I heard today that surprised me: ....

Something I saw today that made me laugh: ....

Something I tasted today that was amazing: ....

Dear Daughter
Rate your day in stars and give it a review
that sounds like a movie review.

EVERYDAY FUN
DAUGHTER

The last place I went: ....

The last photo I took: ....

The last song I heard: ....

The last TV show/movie I watched: ....

What I'm wearing right now: ....

The last person I talked to: ....

The last emoji I used: ....

Something I heard today that surprised me: ....

Something I saw today that made me laugh: ....

Something I tasted today that was amazing: ....

Dear Mom
What's something that happened today
that made you think of me?

....

HELLO, GOODBYE
MOTHER

Someone new in my life that I can't imagine not knowing:

....
....
....
....

A time it was difficult to say goodbye:

....
....
....

What it was like meeting you for the first time:

....
....
....
....

Dear Daughter
Who in our family would you like to learn more about?

HELLO, GOODBYE
DAUGHTER

Someone new in my life that I can't imagine not knowing:

....

....

....

....

A time it was difficult to say goodbye:

....

....

....

Someone I'd like to get to know better:

....

....

....

....

Dear Mom
How did you meet your best friends?

PHOTO MOMENTS
MOTHER

A photo I love and why:

A photo I dislike and why:

Dear Daughter
What photo of you should I keep just between us?

_____

PHOTO MOMENTS
DAUGHTER

A photo I love and why:

A photo I dislike and why:

Dear Mom
What photo would you want framed as a gift?

DAY & NIGHT
MOTHER

My favorite way to start the day:

....
....
....

My favorite way to wind down at night:

....
....
....

My favorite time of day to spend with you:

....
....
....

Dear Daughter
What should we plan for a night out together?

DAY & NIGHT
DAUGHTER

My favorite way to start the day:

....

....

....

My favorite way to wind down at night:

....

....

....

My favorite time of day to spend with you:

....

....

....

Dear Mom
Were you an early bird or a night owl when you were my age?

DATE:

SURVIVAL KIT
MOTHER

Ten things, people, or activities that I could not bear to live a week without:

1. ....

2. ....

3. ....

4. ....

5. ....

6. ....

7. ....

8. ....

9. ....

10. ....

[
Dear Daughter
Do any of our answers match?
]

SURVIVAL KIT
DAUGHTER

Ten things, people, or activities that I could not bear to live a week without:

1. ....

2. ....

3. ....

4. ....

5. ....

6. ....

7. ....

8. ....

9. ....

10. ....

Dear Mom
What different answers would have been on your list as a kid?

MONEY TALK
MOTHER

The longest I have saved for something and what I bought:

....

....

....

....

If I received a gift of $100, here's what I would do with the money:

....

....

....

If I suddenly won a $50,000 prize, here's what I would do with the money:

....

....

....

....

Dear Daughter
If we were to make a donation together,
which charity would you choose?

MONEY TALK
DAUGHTER

The longest I have saved for something and what I bought:

....

....

....

....

If I received a gift of $100, here's what I would do with the money:

....

....

....

If I suddenly won a $50,000 prize, here's what I would do with the money:

....

....

....

....

Dear Mom
What's the first job you had?

SAYING SORRY
MOTHER

A difficult apology I needed to make:

....
....
....

The most meaningful apology I ever received:

....
....
....

Something I need to say sorry to you for:

....
....
....

Dear Daughter
Who was the last person to really hurt your feelings?

SAYING SORRY
DAUGHTER

A difficult apology I needed to make:

....

....

....

....

The most meaningful apology I ever received:

....

....

....

SORRY

Something I need to say sorry to you for:

....

....

....

....

Dear Mom
When were you proud of me for apologizing?

GOOD FRIENDS
MOTHER

My most trusted friends are:

....
....

What brought us close:

....
....
....

What I love about them:

....
....

Dear Daughter

In what ways are you different from your closest friends?

GOOD FRIENDS
DAUGHTER

My most trusted friends are:

....

....

....

What brought us close:

....

....

....

....

What I love about them:

....

....

....

Dear Mom
What did you like to do with your friends when you were my age?

DATE:
_____

DAYDREAM DOODLES
MOTHER

When I let my mind roam free, this is what I doodle:

Dear Daughter
Write a caption for my doodle.

_____

DAYDREAM DOODLES
DAUGHTER

When I let my mind roam free, this is what I doodle:

Dear Mom

Write a caption for my doodle.

FAMOUS FIRSTS
MOTHER

What I remember about our first week together:

....

....

....

What I remember about your first day of school:

....

....

....

....

Another big "first" memory I want to share with you:

....

....

....

Dear Daughter
What next "first" are you looking forward to?

FAMOUS FIRSTS
DAUGHTER

The earliest memory I have:

....
....
....

What I remember about my first day of school:

....
....
....
....

Another big "first" memory I have:

....
....
....

Dear Mom
What next "first" are you excited for me to experience?

MEMBERS ONLY
MOTHER

The clubs, teams, groups, and organizations I've belonged to:

....
....
....
....

The group I've enjoyed the most:

....
....

Ones I'd still like to join:

....
....
....
....

Dear Daughter
Did any of these surprise you?

MEMBERS ONLY
DAUGHTER

The clubs, teams, groups, and organizations I've belonged to:

....

....

....

....

The group I've enjoyed the most:

....

....

Ones I'd still like to join:

....

....

....

....

Dear Mom
What future group do you see me as part of?

BRAVE FACE
MOTHER

One of my most embarrassing moments:

....
....
....
....

Something I would do if I knew I couldn't fail:

....
....
....

What makes me feel brave:

....
....
....
....

Dear Daughter
How can I encourage you?

BRAVE FACE
DAUGHTER

One of my most embarrassing moments:

....

....

....

....

Something I would do if I knew I couldn't fail:

....

....

....

girl **HERO**

What makes me feel brave:

....

....

....

....

Dear Mom
When is a time you've seen me being brave?

DATE:

LOVING TOUCHES
MOTHER

Something I love to touch or feel on my skin:

....
....
....

My favorite ways to show physical affection:

....
....
....

My favorite ways to receive physical affection:

....
....
....

Dear Daughter
Is there anything I do that embarrasses you?

76

LOVING TOUCHES
DAUGHTER

Something I love to touch or feel on my skin:

My favorite ways to show physical affection:

My favorite ways to receive physical affection:

Dear Mom
How did your family share affection when you were growing up?

FREE TIME
MOTHER

If I could spend an entire day outdoors doing anything, I would

....

....

....

....

If I could spend an entire day indoors doing anything, I would

....

....

....

....

My favorite way to waste time is

....

....

....

....

imagine

(**Dear Daughter**
Do you feel like you have enough free time?)

FREE TIME
DAUGHTER

If I could spend an entire day outdoors doing anything, I would

....

....

....

....

If I could spend an entire day indoors doing anything, I would

....

....

....

....

My favorite way to waste time is

....

....

....

....

NICE!

(Dear Mom
What's a pretty perfect day you've had?)

PET PEEVES
MOTHER

Ten things that really annoy me:

1. ....

2. ....

3. ....

4. ....

5. ....

6. ....

7. ....

8. ....

9. ....

10. ....

Dear Daughter
Put a checkmark next to ones that you agree with

PET PEEVES
DAUGHTER

Ten things that really annoy me:

1. ....

2. ....

3. ....

4. ....

5. ....

6. ....

7. ....

8. ....

9. ....

10. ....

Dear Mom
Put a checkmark next to ones that you agree with.

PRIZED POSSESSIONS
MOTHER

Something that was important to me when I was a kid:

....

....

....

Something that's sentimental to me now:

....

....

....

Something from your childhood that I hope you'll always hold on to:

....

....

....

Dear Daughter
Is there something of mine that you'd like me to
pass on to you someday?

PRIZED POSSESSIONS
DAUGHTER

Something that was important to me when I was younger:

....

....

....

Something that's sentimental to me now:

....

....

....

Something I would be mad if you ever got rid of:

....

....

....

Dear Mom
Tell me the story of how you got _____.

SCORING CHORES
MOTHER

A chore I actually don't mind doing:

....

....

....

....

The chore I hate the most:

....

....

....

Where I feel like I could use more help:

....

....

....

....

Dear Daughter
Is there a chore you enjoy doing together with me?

SCORING CHORES
DAUGHTER

A chore I actually don't mind doing:

....

....

....

....

The chore I hate the most:

....

....

....

How I feel about how our family assigns chores:

....

....

....

....

Dear Mom
Is there a chore you enjoy doing together with me?

DATE:

FEELING GRATEFUL
MOTHER

Ten things I'm grateful for right now:

1. ....

2. ....

3. ....

4. ....

5. ....

6. ....

7. ....

8. ....

9. ....

10. ....

Dear Daughter
Put a heart next to ones you relate to.

FEELING GRATEFUL
DAUGHTER

Ten things I'm grateful for right now:

1.
2.
3.
4.
5.
6.
7.
8.
9.
10.

Dear Mom
Put a heart next to ones you relate to.

SPECIAL PROJECTS
MOTHER

DATE:

My favorite school project you worked on:

....

....

....

One of your drawings or writings I've saved:

Where I see you working hard:

....

....

Dear Daughter

Is there any area at school that you need help with?

SPECIAL PROJECTS
DAUGHTER

My favorite school project:

....

....

....

A drawing or writing I've saved:

A school achievement I'm proud of:

....

....

Dear Mom
What areas did you struggle with when you were in school?

GOOD VIBES
MOTHER

Ten random things (foods, songs, etc.) that always give me good vibes:

1. ....

2. ....

3. ....

4. ....

5. ....

6. ....

7. ....

8. ....

9. ....

10. ....

(*Dear Daughter*
How can I help you when you're in a bad mood?)

GOOD VIBES
DAUGHTER

Ten random things (foods, songs, etc.) that always give me good vibes:

1.

2.

3.

4.

5.

6.

7.

8.

9.

10.

Dear Mom
How can I help you when you're in a bad mood?

STARRING ROLES
MOTHER

What I love about being your mother:

....
....
....
....

My toughest challenges as a parent right now:

....
....
....
....

One serious question I want to ask you:

....
....
....
....

Dear Daughter
Please answer the question above honestly.

STARRING ROLES
DAUGHTER

What I love about being your daughter:

....

....

....

....

My toughest challenges in growing up so far:

....

....

....

....

One serious question I want to ask you:

....

....

....

....

Dear Mom
Please answer the question above honestly.

YOU & ME

MOTHER

What I love about our relationship:

....
....
....

What I think we could work on:

....
....
....

How we could grow closer:

....
....
....

Dear Daughter

What did you learn through this journal?

YOU & ME
DAUGHTER

What I love about our relationship:

....

....

....

What I think we could work on:

....

....

....

How we could grow closer:

....

....

....

Dear Mom
What did you learn through this journal?

THIS IS US

Our serious side:

LET'S
GROW

Our silly side: